FRIGHTENED!

Published in paperback in 2019 by Wayland

Text copyright © Wayland 2017
Illustrations copyright © Mike Gordon 2017

Wayland
Carmelite House
50 Victoria Embankment
London EC4Y 0DZ

Wayland Australia
Level 17/207 Kent Street
Sydney, NSW 2000

Managing editor: Victoria Brooker
Creative design: Paul Cherrill

ISBN: 978 1 5263 0078 2

Printed in China

MIX
Paper from
responsible sources
FSC® C104740
FSC
www.fsc.org

Wayland is a division of
Hachette Children's Books,
an Hachette UK company.
www.hachette.co.uk

Feeling FRIGHTENED!

Written by
Kay Barnham

Illustrated by
Mike Gordon

WAYLAND

Something was wrong with Theo. Instead of kicking a football around the playground, he was just leaning against a wall. When Danny got close, he could see that his best friend was actually trembling.
"Are you ill?" asked Danny.
"Shall I take you to the school nurse?"

"Yes, *please*," groaned Theo.
"Then I won't have to do this stupid
talk in front of the class."

"What's the talk about?" asked Danny.
    "Fast cars," said Theo.

"But you know loads about them," said Danny, surprised. "What's the problem?"

6

"I'm *frightened*, OK!" snapped Theo.
"What if I make a mistake?"

"What if I get everything wrong?
What if everyone *laughs* at me?"

"I know," Danny said. "Why don't you practise the talk in front of me?

I won't laugh if you get anything wrong. Then, when you do your talk, you'll know exactly what to say." Theo shrugged. "All right," he said. So he did.

When he spoke in front of the class, Theo's voice
trembled at first. But his talk was great.
"Phew!" he said to Danny. "That was easier than
I thought. I feel great now. When can I do it again?!"

That evening, there was a thunderstorm.

Lightning FLASHED!

Thunder BOOMED!

After a really loud roll of thunder,
Danny heard a small sob.
It was his sister, Rosie. She was hiding
behind the sofa, crying softly.

"Hey," said Danny, crouching down beside his sister, "do you know what thunder and lightning really is?"

Rosie shook her head.
"Not really," she whispered.
"I just know that I'm frightened
and that I want the storm
to STOP."

"When ice, hail and rain in storm clouds rub together, they make a lot of electricity," Danny said. "Lightning is the flash that happens when the electricity jumps about."

"What about thunder?" asked Rosie.

"That's just the sound the lightning makes," explained Danny. "It happens afterwards because light travels much faster than sound."

"It's dangerous to stand under a tree or in
a big open space in a storm. But here is fine.
Come on, let's watch it through the window."
Right then, a zigzag of lightning lit the sky.
"Wow!" gasped Rosie. "That's amazing!"

At the weekend, Danny decided
to visit his grandad, who lived
in the next street.
"Do you want to come?"
he asked his friend, Manish.
"Grandad has lots of sweets,"
he added, with a wink.

"But doesn't he have a dog, too?" asked Manish. Danny nodded. "He's called Barney. He's COOL."

"Oh," said Manish, his face falling.

"Don't you like dogs?" asked Danny, puzzled.

"Not really," replied Manish. "They frighten me a bit."

"Some dogs can be loud and scary at first," said Danny. "But Barney's a lovely dog. He never growls and he doesn't bark much either. Actually, the worst you can expect is a good licking."
"I'm still not sure," said Manish.
"Come on, I'll introduce you!" said Danny.

Danny's grandad opened the door.
"Hi, lads!" he said, grinning widely. Barney
stood at his feet, wagging its tail furiously.
"Be warned, Manish," he said.
"This is the daftest dog
you will ever meet."

At first, Manish stayed away from Barney.
But after watching Danny play with him,
he bravely tried stroking his back.
"See?" said Danny. "Dogs aren't so bad
when you get to know them."
And Manish laughed, as Barney licked his hand.

But that night, it was Danny's turn to be frightened. He lay in bed thinking of the spooky film he'd seen that afternoon. In the film, there were monsters hiding under the bed.
What if there were monsters hiding under *his* bed?

"ARRRGHHHH!"

whispered Danny
in a very small
voice, in case
the monsters
heard him.

And even though moonlight shone outside,
it was so, so dark in Danny's bedroom.
Shadows of ogres and giants loomed
on the wall, swaying to and fro.

Danny didn't
think he
would ever
get to sleep.

Danny hid under the covers, hugging his teddy tightly. Then he began to think of Theo, Rosie and Manish. They'd all been frightened of something, like he was now.

So if he could make them feel better,
was there any reason he couldn't make
himself feel better too ...? Taking a deep breath,
Danny grabbed the torch on his bedside table
and shone it bravely under the bed.
All he could see was a pile of board games.
There wasn't a single monster.

Next, he pulled back the curtains and saw
a tall tree swaying in the wind.
It was making the
shadows on Danny's
wall, not ogres
and giants.

Danny smiled and switched off his torch.
Now that he knew there was nothing
to be frightened about, perhaps
he would go to sleep after all.

FURTHER INFORMATION

THINGS TO DO

1. There is a famous painting by Edvard Munch called
The Scream. Can you draw or paint a picture
of someone looking just as frightened?

2. HELP! EEK! ARGH!
Words and sounds like these can show that someone
is frightened. How many more can you think of?
Can you invent any new ones?

3. Make a colourful word cloud! Start with 'frightened',
then add any other words this makes you think of. Write them
all down using different coloured pens. More important words
should be bigger, less important words smaller.
Start like this...

SCARED
rervous **afraid** fearful

NOTES FOR PARENTS AND TEACHERS

The aim of this book is to help children think about their feelings in an enjoyable, interactive way. Encourage them to have fun pointing to the illustrations, making sounds and acting, too. Here are more specific ideas for getting more out of this book:

1. Encourage children to talk about their own feelings, if they feel comfortable doing so, either while you are reading the book or afterwards. Here are some conversation prompts to try:

What makes you feel frightened?
How do you stop feeling frightened when this happens?

2. Make a facemask that shows a frightened expression.

3. Put on a feelings play! Ask groups of children to act out the different scenarios in the book. The children could use their facemasks to show when they are frightened in the play.

4. Hold a frightening-face competition. Who can look the MOST scary? Strictly no laughing allowed!

BOOKS TO SHARE

A Book of Feelings
by Amanda McCardie, illustrated by Salvatore Rubbino
(Walker, 2016)

Frog is Frightened
by Max Velthuijs
(Andersen Press, 2014)

I Feel Frightened
by Brian Moses, illustrated by Mike Gordon
(Wayland, 1994)

Samuel Scaredosaurus (Dinosaurs Have Feelings, Too)
by Brian Moses, illustrated by Mike Gordon
(Wayland, 2015)

The Great Big Book of Feelings
by Mary Hoffman, illustrated by Ros Asquith
(Frances Lincoln, 2016)

The Owl Who Was Afraid of the Dark
by Jill Tomlinson, illustrated by Paul Howard
(Egmont, 2014)